WITHDRAWN

NATIVE AMERICAN LEGENDS

RED CLOUD

Don McLeese

Rourke
Publishing LLC
Vero Beach, Florida 32964

www.rourkepublishing.com

PHOTO CREDITS:
©Library of Congress Cover, Title, pgs 5, 6, 9, 13, 23, 26
©Hulton/Archive by Getty Images pgs 10, 15, 16, 19, 21
©James P. Rowan pg 24

Title page: *Chief Red Cloud in a photo taken around 1901*

Editor: Frank Sloan

Cover and page design by Nicola Stratford

Library of Congress Cataloging-in-Publication Data

McLeese, Don.
  Red Cloud / Don McLeese.
      p. cm. -- (Native American legends)
Summary: A brief biography of the famous leader of the Oglala Sioux who led his people to victory against the United States Army at the Battle of Fort Phil Kearny.
Includes bibliographical references and index.
  ISBN 1-58952-727-5 (hardcover)
 1. Red Cloud, 1822-1909--Juvenile literature. 2. Oglala
Indians--Kings and rulers--Biography--Juvenile literature. 3. Red
Cloud's War, 1866-1867--Juvenile literature. [1. Red Cloud, 1822-1909.
2. Oglala Indians--Biography. 3. Indians of North America--Biography. 4.
Kings, queens, rulers, etc.] I. Title. II. Series.
  E99.O3R376 2003
  978.004'9752--dc21

                                                    2003004372

Printed in the USA

w/w

Table of Contents

There were many chiefs of Native American **tribes** who were also brave **warriors**. But only one of them won a war against the United States government. This was Red Cloud, **chief** of the **Lakota Sioux** tribe known as the **Oglala**.

Native Americans had lived in the land that is now the United States for hundreds of years before white **settlers** went there. The Native Americans believed that no one could own the land, that it belonged to everyone. The white people who came from Europe to make a new country wanted to own the land.

Two Lakota women (standing) and a Lakota man on horseback. ➤
One of the women is holding an infant in a cradleboard.

The settlers wanted to move the Native Americans away from the land where they had always lived. They fought battles and killed many of the Native Americans who wouldn't leave. The United States had more soldiers and more guns than the Native American warriors. The soldiers lost some battles to Native American tribes, but almost always won the wars.

Red Cloud, however, wouldn't give up. When the United States tried to take away the Sioux land where he lived, he and his tribe fought back. It was the United States that finally gave up. Its soldiers left the land where Red Cloud lived. Red Cloud had won this war!

◄ *A young Oglala girl sits in front of a tipi.*

Red Cloud's Childhood

Red Cloud was born in 1822. His Sioux name was "Makhpiya-Luta." He lived in what is now western Nebraska, near the Platte River. This was good land for hunting and for fishing, which is how the tribe fed itself. Red Cloud's mother was a member of the Oglala Sioux tribe. His father was a member of a different tribe.

Not much is known about Red Cloud's boyhood, except that his father died when Red Cloud was very young. The man who took the place of his father in his life was his mother's brother, Chief Smoke. He was the leader of his tribe, and he was Red Cloud's uncle.

A photograph of an Oglala mother carrying her child on her back ➤

Like other Sioux boys, Red Cloud played games as a child that would help teach him to become a great warrior. He also learned and loved the stories of the Sioux. He became a great speaker, someone who told stories very well.

Platte River
It starts in the mountains of Colorado, and it is the biggest river in what is now Nebraska. Red Cloud was born near what is now the city of North Platte in western Nebraska.

◅ *A painting of Native Americans and settlers meeting at a trading camp near the Platte River*

There were a lot of fights with other Native American tribes when Red Cloud was growing up. The Oglala tribe that Chief Smoke led often fought with another tribe, the Koya Oglalas. The leader of that tribe was Chief Bull Bear.

When Red Cloud was 19 years old, there was a battle in 1841 between the two tribes. Red Cloud had become a great warrior. He won the battle for his tribe by killing Chief Bull Bear, his uncle's enemy. It was plain that Red Cloud was no longer a boy.

The next year, he became leader of the Oglala warriors when they went into battle. He also became a husband in 1842 when he married Pretty Owl.

A painting showing a battle between Sioux and Blackfeet Indians ➤

Settlers Go West

When the United States became a country in 1776, there were only 13 states. These were on the east coast, at the edge of the Atlantic Ocean. To the west was land, thousands of miles of it, which went all the way to the Pacific Ocean. Native Americans had long lived on this land, which white people called the **frontier**.

The United States soon wanted to have more land for more states, so white settlers started moving west. As they did, they built houses, started villages, and said that the land was theirs.

Pioneers cross the Plains westward in a wagon train. ➤

The Native Americans didn't like this, because they believed the land was for the use of everyone. Sometimes the Native Americans and the white settlers made peace and became friends. Other times they fought. More white settlers kept moving farther and farther west.

"Westward, Ho!"
This means "Let's go west!" The settlers would shout this as they began their journey.

Sharing the Land

By the 1850s, white settlers had begun to make their way to the land that is now Nebraska, South Dakota, and Wyoming. Many Native Americans lived on this land, including Red Cloud's tribe. The white settlers began building **forts**, with big walls to protect against attacks.

Instead of fighting, the white settlers and Native Americans tried to find a way to get along. In 1851, the two sides agreed to sign a piece of paper, called a **treaty**. The treaty said that the Native Americans would continue to let white settlers pass through this land and go west, without the Native Americans trying to stop them. The United States would then pay money to the Native Americans for letting them travel on the land.

Fort Laramie
This was one of the busiest centers for trading between white settlers and Native Americans. It is still one of the most important sites for history in Wyoming and is open to the public.

◄ *Traders, soldiers, and Native Americans gather at Fort Laramie.*

Gold

During the 1860s, a lot more white settlers than ever before went west through Native American territory. A metal called gold had been found in what is now Montana, and it was worth a lot of money. The white people wanted to own the gold and own the land.

The Montana Gold Rush
In 1862, gold was found in land that is now the southwest part of Montana. Lots of people rushed from the east to try to find more of it. This was called a "gold rush."

A Native American chief forbids the passage of a wagon train through his land.

The Native Americans didn't trust the white people. The tribes knew that other tribes had been made to leave land where they had long lived because the white people moved there. Red Cloud knew that he and his warriors would have to fight to keep the land where they lived.

Forts and Battles

The white settlers were also getting ready to fight. The army built a series of forts along what was called the Bozeman Trail. This trail went through Native American territory to Montana. The soldiers killed hundreds of Native Americans in battles.

Beginning in 1866, Red Cloud and other warriors began attacking groups of travelers who were heading toward Montana for gold.

The Bozeman Trail
This trail was 600 miles (966 kilometers) long and went from Fort Laramie to what is now Montana. It was started by John M. Bozeman in 1863.

Settlers defend Fort Union. ➤

The Native Americans also began attacking the forts, where soldiers would shoot back at them. Red Cloud hoped that the white settlers would be afraid to live in this Native American territory.

The Battle of Fort Phil Kearny

In December of 1866, Red Cloud and his warriors won a big battle in what is now Wyoming, one of the most important victories ever for Native Americans. They surrounded Fort Phil Kearny. Inside the walls of the fort were Captain William Fetterman and 80 soldiers. Red Cloud wouldn't let the soldiers leave and wouldn't let anyone into the fort to give food or weapons to the soldiers. Because Red Cloud had the soldiers trapped, his warriors won the big battle.

Fort Phil Kearny
This fort in what is now northeastern Wyoming was named for a Civil War general. It is open to the public and has a museum.

Two Oglala chiefs: American Horse (left) and Red Cloud (right) ➤

No. 3691. "Red Cloud and American Horse.
The two most noted Chiefs now living. Photo and
copyright '91 by Grabill. P. & V. C. Deadwood

The Fort Laramie Treaty

This big victory ended a war between Red Cloud's tribe and the United States. Both sides went back to Fort Laramie in 1868 and signed another treaty. The United States agreed to leave the forts it had built along the Bozeman Trail.

The treaty said that this land in what is now South Dakota, Wyoming, and Montana belonged to the Sioux. It said that the Sioux had been right to stay on the land and the white settlers were wrong in trying to take it away from them. The treaty said that the white people would build no more roads through the land of the Sioux.

◄ *A recent photograph of buildings taken at the Fort Laramie National Historical Site*

A Peaceful Chief

There would continue to be fighting between the U.S. soldiers and Native Americans, but Red Cloud was done fighting. After winning the war and signing the treaty, he wanted peace. In 1870, he traveled to Washington, D.C., so that Native Americans could trade for things they needed at Fort Laramie. He lived until 1909. Since his death, he has been remembered as the only Native American chief to win a war against the United States.

◄ *A photograph of Red Cloud as an old man.*

Red Cloud's People

Red Cloud was a chief of a Lakota Sioux tribe known as the Oglala. The large Lakota Sioux were sometimes known just as the Sioux. They moved around from the plains of what is now Nebraska to the Black Hills of land that is now South Dakota.

Today's Oglala are part of the Teton Sioux, which is divided into seven bands. About 60,000 of them live on reservations in South Dakota. Some also live in the Canadian province of Saskatchewan.

Time Line

1776	The United States becomes a country.
1822	Red Cloud is born.
1841	Red Cloud kills Chief Bull Bear.
1842	Red Cloud marries Pretty Owl.
1851	A treaty is signed that allows white settlers to pass through Native American land.
1862	Gold is found in Montana.
1863	Bozeman Trail is started.
1866	Red Cloud wins battle of Fort Phil Kearny.
1868	The Fort Laramie Treaty is signed.
1870	Red Cloud travels to Washington, D.C.
1909	Red Cloud dies.

Glossary

chief (CHEEF) — leader, head of a Native American tribe

forts (FORTZ) — places protected by big walls where soldiers and people lived. Some forts were the size of a small village

frontier (frun TEER) — a wilderness that has yet to be settled

Lakota Sioux (lah KOH tuh SUU) — a tribe of Native Americans, sometimes just called "Sioux"

Native Americans (NAY tiv uh MARE ih cans) — those who lived in the land that is now the United States before explorers from Europe came

Oglala (Ohg LAH luh) — a Lakota Sioux tribe that lived in what is now Nebraska and South Dakota

settlers (SET lers) — people who move to a new land to live there

treaty (TREE tee) — a paper that people sign that says they agree to something

tribes (TRYBZ) — the bands or nations of Native Americans

warriors (WAHR ee urz) — great fighters in battle

Further Reading

Freedman, Russell. *Indian Chiefs*. Holiday House, 1989

Lazer, Jerry. *Red Cloud: Sioux War Chief*. Chelsea House, 1995

Sanford, William R. *Red Cloud, Sioux Warrior*. Enslow Publishers, Inc. 1994

Websites to Visit

www.pbs.org/weta/thewest/people/i_r/redcloud.htm

www.ilhawaii.net/~stony/redcloud.html

jbtank.com/indians/redcloud.html

Index

About The Author

Don McLeese is an award-winning journalist whose work has appeared in many newspapers and magazines. He earned his M.A. degree in English from the University of Chicago, taught feature writing at the University of Texas and has frequently contributed to the World Book Encyclopedia. He lives with his wife and two daughters in West Des Moines, Iowa.